Many Blessings,

Rosie

Early Praise *(continued)*

I find myself picking up this book and seeing what page it opens to each day as sort of a divination tool to choose what wisdom to live by for the day. Each tidbit hits right in the center of my soul and my whole being says 'ahh, yes, this is the truth you've been hiding from, avoiding, or blind to.' This will be mandatory reading for all of my clients! Thank you Rosie, for this blessing.

~Jessica "Ruby" Hernandez, MFT Intern and Transformational Coach, www.RubyMoonHealingArts.com

*****

Whether she's writing or speaking, **Dr. Rosie** consistently expresses herself in a way that offers accessible insights and Aha Experiences, enriched by her fearless personal revelations. If you can hear her speak, do! She's a life-changer. Read her, taking the time to savor, digest, and allow each profound tidbit the opportunity to reach and awaken your Miraculous Existence.

Virginia Erhardt, Ph.D., Licensed Clinical Psychologist

*****

"Each of the 101 insights that Dr. Kuhn shares are a simple and profound opportunity to reflect and meditate on one's own truth. As I moved thru the book there were joyous moments of the ah-ha's and a sense of being seen. And then there were also the long pauses as the insights drew me into deeper recesses of new discoveries of my being. A desk-side treasure for healers and a bedside support for all on the journey of life.

Lori Pinnell. MA Transpersonal Studies, BMgt, BA, RYT Transformational Life Coach Founder, InnerWorks Consulting

Knowing Rosie these many years in roles such as teacher/student, supervisor/supervisee, friend and colleague, I am so pleased to share her vision for this little book. I say *little* but it is a book of such weight! Rosie is a travelling pioneer. She takes her many tools with her to those interior places as not yet discovered and comes back to us with wisdom to share in memorable truths. I have been living with one page a week on my fridge door and explore it all day long. The reader will find their own manner of study and absorption.

Gloria Taylor, CT Consulting, Lifestreams Counselling Centre, Waterloo Lutheran Seminary

*****

Dr. Rosie Kuhn has done it again with book 3 of her 101 series. She has captured the spiritual issues that are never discussed in therapy but should be. Her new book, "101 Indispensable Insights I Didn't Get In Therapy", is a must read, that can be kept on the bedside table for easy reference. Through her own suffering she came to an epiphany, she was more than emotions, thoughts and sensations, she needed to address the spiritual aspects of our human experience! Life is messy at times and creates separation, but these 101 insights bring us back to ourselves and help us to reconnect with our *True Nature*.

David Bennett, Author of "Voyage of Purpose: Spiritual Wisdom from Near-Death back to Life"

******

This is a delightful book, blessed with wisdom, wit and brevity. My favorites include #37, #38, (most favorite), # 41, #58 and # 80. I'm still smiling from reading it.

James Fadiman, Ph.D, Co-founder, Institute for Transpersonal Psychology, Author, "Unlimit Your Life".

******

Dr. Rosie Kuhn's 101 insights are truly indispensable; each one is a gem to be savored time and time again. They resonate with my own experiences and the experiences of others with whom I have journeyed on their human/spiritual path.

Written with intelligence, simplicity, wisdom, humor and most essentially, truth, it seems evident to me that Rosie has tapped into the Great Truth or Reality of God.

This is the best personal growth book that I have ever read and I highly recommend it to all. Allow yourself time to read the Dedication and Introduction, both a "taste" of what is to follow, and what follows may just transform your life!"

Marilyn Granucci, Spiritual Director and Retreat Leader, Mercy Center, Burlingame, CA.

******

When your time is precious, its books like *ME...* that are a perfect fit for the overwhelmed, busy people who have just a brief moment to pause and let in some truth and grace.

"Dr. Rosie is the needed answer to a problem no one is talking about. There has been a blatant lack of support that bridges the gap between our mind and our spirit. While many people seek spirituality in their spare time, while regularly visiting their therapist to work on their "real" problems, Dr. Rosie shows us that it is all spiritual and all real; it is all human and no on-the-side stuff. Taking these 101 powerful insights in, I started to see my life and my world with fresh eyes. I started to feel the relief I was seeking. This book contains simple solutions to complicated problems in nice, digestible morsels - Juicy, jam packed realizations without long, drawn out explanations. An enjoyable, insightful read!"

Jenna Smith, Ontological Coach & Spiritual Psychotherapist, www.jenna.to

ME...

101
INDISPENSABLE
INSIGHTS
I DIDN'T GET
IN THERAPY

ROSIE KUHN, PH.D.

ISBN: 978-0-9908151-0-5

ACKNOWLEDGMENTS

I am deeply grateful to have been blessed, again and again with phenomenal learning environments, clearly beyond the bandwidth of most training programs for psychotherapists. Among these were: *Interfaith Pastoral Counselling Center* in Kitchener, Ontario Canada; *California Family Study Center*, (now *Phillips Graduate Institute*, Chatsworth, CA); and, *The Institute of Transpersonal Psychology*, (now *Sofia University*, Palo Alto, CA). Each of these provided me with an approach to psychotherapy that included both a spiritual and transpersonal orientation. Through these programs, I was presented with opportunities to train with individuals who had a larger vision than most psychotherapeutic practitioners and facilities. I am deeply indebted to each of my instructors for their invitation into a more expansive arena of life as a human being. Thank you for gifting me with the tools that have allowed me to engage in the incredible relationships I now share with my clients.

DEDICATION

Rarely do we address spiritual issues within the psychotherapy session. The truth is, however, that spiritual issues are the foundational determinant of all human suffering, which is precisely what brings people into the offices of professional psycho-therapists and healers in the first place. Yet, most people decline to discuss the spiritual underpinnings of their problems. I didn't get the importance of this through my therapy training. I just didn't get it.

What I did "get", I got from working with my clients, who were and *are* my teachers and guides, mentoring me to follow, and at the same time, direct them into the fullest and most raw expression of their essential, spiritual selves. My clients ask me to take their hand and steward them along the rocky road of the evolution of their human spirit. When I hesitate, they hesitate. When I trust them to go deeper, they go deeper.

Ongoingly, these daring individuals require of me that I cultivate awareness, curiosity and presence, to greater and greater degrees. In doing this, I become a clearer reflection for their own truths, their own dilemmas and hesitations, for their courage and their ability to change the things they can, to surrender when they can't, and to discern for themselves which is in their highest truth.

Each one of my clients teaches me that, without curiosity and presence, I'm disconnected, and I miss out on an exquisite opportunity to truly know another, and to truly know myself.

With that in mind, I dedicate this book to my clients, for they have given me these gifts, the value of which is beyond measure. Because of these gifts, I am a better person in the world. With deep gratitude, I acknowledge you as my finest teachers.

I NEVER GOT
IN THERAPY THAT...

INTRODUCTION

Psychotherapy, Psychology, Psychiatry. Each profession was created to support and empower individuals to develop a personal, intimate relationship with their Psyche, that is to say, their *Soul*, their *Spirit*, their *Essence* their *Consciousness*, their *Inner Self*.

The truth is, that it is the rare therapist that has plummeted to the depths required of them to support clients in engaging directly with their psyche. I know. I trained as a therapist and have my Ph.D. in Transpersonal Psychology, so I'm not speaking about *them*. I am, in many ways, one of *them*, and in other ways, I am something else too. That *something else* has allowed me to cross a threshold into a larger bandwidth of human reality.

It wasn't until my first real job, working with people in recovery, that I came upon what I consider to be the essential ingredient to human growth and development: Spirituality.

Throughout my doctorate program, I specialized in the field of Spiritual Guidance, in service to my desire to integrate spirituality into a therapeutic practice. My training in Ontological Coaching became the conduit for all of the skills and tools I developed in psychotherapy, spiritual guidance and life coaching. Ontological Coaching was where the synthesis happened.

Now, as a Transformational Life Coach, my work differs from both the work I did as a therapist, and my work as a spiritual guide. What I didn't get in therapy is that there is a ME beyond who I thought myself to be. I didn't get in therapy that the "ME in me" is *Miraculous Existence*.

Under normal circumstances, the elements of spirituality are all but cast out of a therapy session. In therapy, we acknowledge the emotions, thoughts and sensations of our bodies, but we don't address the indispensable *Spiritual* aspect of the human experience, without which we would not exist.

This human dilemma in which we find ourselves is wrought with experiences that are beyond cognitive understanding. It is likely that each one of us will experience unspeakable, numinous, transformative and spiritual experiences, and never know what to call them, or worse, how to be with them. Too often, our priests, ministers and rabbis are also befuddled by our human experiences; often the very experiences that connect us to our spirituality.

Challenges occur that make no sense to us. We become confused and frustrated and we begin to wonder "Am I normal?". We become depressed and beat ourselves up, simply because we don't have the capacity to understand and deal with situations with the tools we have at hand.

As a Transformational LIFE Coach, my job is to empower people to be in their LIFE consciously. I ask questions that require my clients to be in direct experience with their reality, with their thoughts and emotions. With this level of mindfullness, they come to know what is true and how to be, based on their own truth, not that of consensus realty. I didn't learn how to do this in therapy, not as the therapist, nor as a client.

A few months ago, while in the midst of a spiritual crisis, in the midst of incredible angst and agony, I had an epiphany. I said to myself: "I never 'got it' from therapy, that what I am going through right now, is an inevitable part of being a spiritual being having a human experience." In that moment, I was inspired to write *101 Indispensable Insights That I Didn't Get In Therapy*.

I openly share with you, too, that there are many therapists and clients who *did* get these insights through therapy. I admit, that possibly I wasn't ready, open, or perhaps listening when these insights crossed my path. I didn't get it then; but I certainly get it now!

I NEVER GOT
IN THERAPY THAT...

I AM A SPIRITUAL BEING,
FIRST & FOREMOST.
SOMETIMES I NEED SUPPORT
IN FIGURING OUT
HOW TO BE A HUMAN BEING
& A SPIRITUAL BEING
ALL AT THE SAME TIME.

#1

I NEVER GOT
IN THERAPY THAT...

I'M NOT HERE
TO BE NORMAL.
I'M HERE TO BE
A UNIQUE WORK OF ART.

#2

I NEVER GOT
IN THERAPY THAT...

I'M HERE TO
LEARN HOW TO
BE ME*
WITHIN MY HUMANNESS,
IN A SELF-HONORING WAY.

*AKA, MIRACULOUS EXISTENCE.

#3

I NEVER GOT
IN THERAPY THAT...

I HAVE AN INTELLIGENCE
THAT I RARELY USE
WHEN IT COMES
TO PERCEIVED REALITY,
EMOTIONS & BODY SENSATIONS.
NO ONE SEEMS TO WANT ME
TO KNOW THIS ABOUT MYSELF.

#4

I NEVER GOT
IN THERAPY THAT...

MOST OF MY PROBLEMS
STEM FROM THE FACT
THAT I DON'T WANT TO GROW UP;
I DON'T WANT TO BE RESPONSIBLE;
& SOMETIMES I'M NOT EVEN
SURE I WANT TO BE HERE!

#5

I NEVER GOT
IN THERAPY THAT...

GUILT IMPOSES CONTROL
BY MAKING PEOPLE WRONG & BAD.
I DON'T HAVE TO FEEL GUILTY,
BECAUSE TRUTHFULLY,
I RARELY DO THINGS THAT
ARE WRONG OR BAD;
I'M JUST AFRAID THEY
MIGHT BE PERCEIVED AS SO.

#6

I NEVER GOT
IN THERAPY THAT...

THERE IS NOTHING WRONG
WITH ME FOR FEELING
HOPELESS, POWERLESS & HELPLESS.
IN FACT, THERE MAY BE
SOMETHING WRONG WITH ME,
IF, FROM TIME-TO-TIME, I DON'T.

#7

I NEVER GOT
IN THERAPY THAT...

ONLY A SMALL PERCENTAGE
OF THE POPULATION
REALLY HAS MENTAL DISORDERS.
THE REST OF US ARE JUST
HIDING OUT, TERRIFIED TO FACE
OUR MAGNIFICENT SELVES.

#8

I NEVER GOT
IN THERAPY THAT...

WHEN I HAVE THE THOUGHT,
"THIS ISN'T HOW MY LIFE
IS SUPPOSED TO LOOK",
I AM JOLTED TO REMEMBER,
"THIS IS EXACTLY
HOW MY LIFE
IS SUPPOSED TO LOOK."

#9

I NEVER GOT
IN THERAPY THAT...

LIFE IS MESSY & RAW.
ATTEMPTING TO REMAIN
INVULNERABLE TO IT
ONLY MINIMIZES
MY EXPERIENCE OF
THE RAPTURE
& EXQUISITE BEAUTY
I AM HERE TO EXPERIENCE.

#10

I NEVER GOT
IN THERAPY THAT...

MY SPIRITUAL LIFE
IS MY PERSONAL LIFE,
IS MY HUMAN LIFE,
IS THE WORK I DO IN THE WORLD.
I AM NEVER SEPARATED FROM
ME*.

*MIRACULOUS EXISTENCE.

#11

I NEVER GOT
IN THERAPY THAT...

THE MAJORITY OF
MY LIFE DILEMMAS
ARE CAUSED
BY IGNORING MY OWN
SPIRITUAL PRINCIPLES.
WHAT ARE THEY AGAIN?

#12

I NEVER GOT
IN THERAPY THAT...

TO HAVE A GREAT LIFE,
I'M REQUIRED TO,
AT LEAST SOMETIMES, SHED A LOT
OF BLOOD, SWEAT & TEARS.
WELL, MAYBE NOT
SO MUCH BLOOD.

#13

I NEVER GOT
IN THERAPY THAT...

THE GRIEF PROCESS
IS ONE OF THE MOST ESSENTIAL
COMPONENTS OF HEALTHY LIVING.
IT REQUIRES CONSTANT
AWARENESS OF THE REALIZATION
THAT I AM SURRENDERING
MY EXISTENCE
IN EVERY MOMENT.

#14

I NEVER GOT
IN THERAPY THAT...

SELF-ACKNOWLEDGMENT
IS THE BEGINNING
OF SELF-ACCEPTANCE,
SELF-RESPECT
& SELF-HONORING BEHAVIOR.
MAYBE, I'LL EVEN COME
TO LOVE MYSELF.

#15

I NEVER GOT
IN THERAPY THAT...

THERE IS ABSOLUTELY
NO LOGICAL REASON
TO STAY IN RELATIONSHIPS
WITH PEOPLE, PLACES & THINGS
THAT BRING HARM &
SUFFERING TO ME.
IT JUST DOESN'T MAKE SENSE.

#16

I NEVER GOT
IN THERAPY THAT...

CHOOSING TO STAY
IN AN ABUSIVE RELATIONSHIP,
ONCE I REALIZE I AM IN ONE,
REQUIRES THAT I BE 100%
RESPONSIBLE FOR THE OUTCOME
OF THAT DECISION.
NO ONE ELSE BUT ME IS
ACCOUNTABLE FOR THE
CONSEQUENCES OF MY CHOICES.

#17

I NEVER GOT
IN THERAPY THAT...

I AM THE CENTER OF MY REALITY.
ALL MY CHOICES ARE BASED
ON ME & MY DESIRES FOR
CONNECTION, SAFETY
& WELL-BEING.
I'M ALWAYS, ALWAYS, ALWAYS
ACTING ON MY OWN BEHALF FIRST,
NO MATTER WHAT.

#18

I NEVER GOT
IN THERAPY THAT...

SELF-EMPOWERMENT IS
THE MOST IMPORTANT
& THE MOST VALUABLE OUTCOME
OF ANY THERAPY.
IF I'M NOT DEVELOPING GREATER
CAPACITIES TO SELF-EMPOWER,
THEN I'M WASTING
MY TIME & MY ENERGY.

#19

I NEVER GOT
IN THERAPY THAT...

THERAPISTS DON'T
KNOW EVERYTHING,
NOR DO THEY HAVE ALL THE
ANSWERS, OR ALL THE TOOLS.
I TRUST MYSELF TO
CHOOSE WHAT & WHO WILL BE THE
BEST RESOURCE, SUPPORT,
& THINKING PARTNER FOR ME.

#20

I NEVER GOT
IN THERAPY THAT...

IF MY THERAPIST SAYS "TRUST ME,"
I HAVE AN OPPORTUNITY
TO FIGURE OUT WHETHER IT'S THE
THERAPIST I AM NEEDING
TO TRUST, OR TO
SIMPLY TRUST MYSELF.

#21

I NEVER GOT
IN THERAPY THAT...

THERE IS A DISTINCTION BETWEEN
WHAT NEEDS TO BE FIXED
& HEALED, & WHAT NEEDS TO
UNFOLD ORGANICALLY.
A LOT OF MY CHALLENGES ARE JUST
THE NATURAL EVOLUTION
OF MY SELF INTO ME.
NO FIXING REQUIRED!

#22

I NEVER GOT
IN THERAPY THAT...

I NEED TO LEARN
THAT I AM MY OWN BEST FRIEND.
THIS COMES, I THINK,
AFTER I LEARN THAT I'VE BEEN
MY OWN WORST ENEMY
ON MORE THAN ONE OCCASION.

#23

I NEVER GOT
IN THERAPY THAT...

98% OF MY LIFE HAS BEEN LIVED
BASED ON PERCEPTIONS
I'VE CHOSEN TO BELIEVE ARE REAL.
THE ACTUAL THERAPY STARTS
WHEN I BEGIN TO WITNESS WHO
I AM BENEATH THOSE
LAYERS OF BELIEFS & MEMORIES.

#24

I NEVER GOT
IN THERAPY THAT...

RESTLESS, IRRITABLE DISCONTENT
IS TO BE ADDRESSED,
NOT AVOIDED, IGNORED
OR MEDICATED.

#25

I NEVER GOT
IN THERAPY THAT...

RESTLESS, IRRITABLE DISCONTENT
IS NOT CAUSED BY OTHER
PEOPLE OR CIRCUMSTANCES.

#26

I NEVER GOT
IN THERAPY THAT...

RESTLESS, IRRITABLE DISCONTENT
IS AN INNATE HUMAN CONDITION,
WHICH, WHEN ACKNOWLEDGED
& RECOGNIZED FOR WHAT IT IS,
(A CONGLOMERATION
OF BELIEFS THAT MAKE UP
CONSENSUS REALITY),
CAN BE DISCHARGED OF ITS
DUTIES, & ALLOWED TO GO
ON A PERMANENT VACATION.

#27

I NEVER GOT
IN THERAPY THAT...

SPIRITUAL IMMERSION
IS A REQUIRED ENDEAVOR.
TO MEDICATE IT WITH PILLS
WILL ONLY MAINTAIN ITS
PRESENCE, & POSTPONE
THE INEVITABLE EXPERIENCE
OF LIGHT & LOVE.

#28

I NEVER GOT
IN THERAPY THAT...

BECAUSE I EXIST,
CHALLENGES OCCUR. NO FIXING
OR PROBLEM SOLVING REQUIRED.
I CHOOSE TO FIND MY WAY
THROUGH THE MAZE OF BELIEFS &
INTERPRETATIONS, USING ALL THAT
I'VE LEARNED BEFORE THIS MO-
MENT. IF ONLY I COULD
REMEMBER WHAT I'VE LEARNED!

#29

I NEVER GOT
IN THERAPY THAT...

THIS MOMENT ONLY HOLDS
WHAT I BRING INTO IT.
MY PERCEPTIONS ARE
MEMORIES OF THE PAST.
IF THEY DIDN'T SERVE IN THE PAST,
THEY WILL NOT SERVE ME
IN THIS PRESENT MOMENT.

#30

I NEVER GOT
IN THERAPY THAT...

DILEMMAS ARE OPPORTUNITIES
TO DISCERN MY HIGHEST VALUES
& HIGHEST TRUTH.
I CAN THEN CHOOSE TO STEP
LIGHTLY ONLY TOWARDS THAT.

#31

I NEVER GOT
IN THERAPY THAT...

SUSTAINABILITY REQUIRES
TWO STEPS FORWARD &
ONE STEP BACK,
OVER & OVER & OVER AGAIN,
UNTIL I'VE PERMANENTLY ARRIVED.

#32

I NEVER GOT
IN THERAPY THAT...

CELLULAR MEMORY
IS THE DENSE GOOEY STUFF
THAT KEEPS US FROM CREATING
MAGIC & MIRACLES.
PURGING THIS GOO IS REQUIRED.
LIKE ANY DETOXING REMEDY,
IT MAY BE UNCOMFORTABLE &
DISORIENTING FOR A TIME.
INEVITABLY, THE ESSENTIAL ME*
SHINES THROUGH.

*MIRACULOUS EXISTENCE.

#33

I NEVER GOT
IN THERAPY THAT...

DENIAL IS A POWERFUL
PHENOMENON THAT PROTECTS
A FRAGILE IDENTITY
FROM SHATTERING.
IF, AT FIRST, I HONOR THIS
PHENOMENAL TOOL,
IN TIME, DENIAL
BECOMES UNNECESSARY.

#34

I NEVER GOT
IN THERAPY THAT...

MY LIFE IS A TESTIMONY
TO MY CAPACITY TO CHOOSE
IN SERVICE TO MY HIGHEST
TRUTH & MY HIGHEST GOOD.
PERHAPS, AT TIMES,
I'VE LIMITED MYSELF TO TRUTHS
THAT AREN'T QUITE SO TRUE.
I HAVE MORE EXPLORING TO DO.

#35

I NEVER GOT
IN THERAPY THAT...

IN ORDER TO LIVE INTO
& EXPERIENCE THE
FULL POTENTIALITY OF ME,
I AM REQUIRED TO
PRACTICE STRETCHING,
STRENGTHENING,
& INCREASING
THE RANGE OF MOTION OF MY
LEAP-OF-FAITH MUSCLES.

#36

I NEVER GOT
IN THERAPY THAT...

WE ARE ALREADY WHOLE.
THERAPISTS, COACHES
& SPIRITUAL GUIDES ARE STEWARDS
& WITNESSES TO THE WAYS
WE DISREGARD, DENY & IGNORE
OUR WHOLENESS.

#37

I NEVER GOT

IN THERAPY THAT...

D.E.N.I.A.L.

DON'T EVEN KNOW I AM LOVE.

#38

I NEVER GOT
IN THERAPY THAT...

IF I CHOOSE NOT TO PUT
INTO DIRECT PRACTICE
THE INSIGHTS
I RECIEVE FROM MY
MEDITATIONS & PRAYER SESSIONS,
I WILL MERELY CONFIRM
WHAT I KNOW.
I BECOME MORE SELF-REALIZED,
YET NO CLOSER TO EXPERIENCING
THE FULLEST EXPRESSION
OF MY ESSENTIAL NATURE.

#39

I NEVER GOT
IN THERAPY THAT...

RESISTANCE IS A WISE PRACTICE.
IT MAKES SENSE TO STOP,
LOOK, & LISTEN FOR WHAT
I NEED TO SEE, HEAR, & KNOW,
IN ORDER TO STEP DARINGLY
ONTO THE NEXT PIECE OF THE
ROAD I LAY DOWN BEFORE ME.

#40

I NEVER GOT
IN THERAPY THAT...

THE MORE I LAUGH AT MYSELF
& MY CIRCUMSTANCE,
THE MORE I KNOW
I'M GETTING HEALTHIER
& HEALTHIER, & HEALTHIER.

#41

I NEVER GOT
IN THERAPY THAT...

THE PRACTICE AS A THERAPIST
IS TO EMPOWER PEOPLE
TO EMPOWER THEMSELVES
TO TRUST THEIR OWN CAPACITY
TO LIVE A WONDERFUL LIFE.
MANY OF US CAN BE
OUR OWN THERAPISTS!

#42

I NEVER GOT
IN THERAPY THAT...

THE MORE I THINK OF OTHERS
AS INCAPABLE FOOLS,
THE MORE THEY PROVE ME RIGHT.
THE MORE I THINK OF OTHERS
AS BRILLIANT, CREATIVE BEINGS,
THE MORE THEY PROVE ME RIGHT.

#43

I NEVER GOT
IN THERAPY THAT...

ACCOUNTABILITY, OR KARMA,
IS A PRACTICE
TO OVERCOME LIMITED BELIEFS
WHICH HAD ME LIVE
AS IF I HAD A RIGHT
TO HARM MYSELF & OTHERS.

#44

I NEVER GOT
IN THERAPY THAT...

ULTIMATELY,
I AM,
WITH NO PAST & NO FUTURE.
NO STRIVING IS NECESSARY;
I'M ALREADY HERE.

#45

I NEVER GOT
IN THERAPY THAT...

MY MOST WISE & DISCERNING
GUIDES & THINKING PARTNERS
ARE IN THE REALM OF THE UNSEEN.
EVERY RELIGION TELLS US THIS, YET
MAKES US FEEL CRAZY
WHEN WE TALK ABOUT IT.
WHAT'S UP WITH THAT?

#46

I NEVER GOT
IN THERAPY THAT...

I AM HERE TO LEARN
BALANCED PARTNERSHIP,
NOT DEPENDENCE.
BELIEVING I NEED TO LEAN ON
OTHERS CREATES IMBALANCE.

#47

I NEVER GOT
IN THERAPY THAT...

I TRUST THAT
I AM TRUSTWORTHY.
I TRUST MY CAPACITY TO TRUST.
I TRUST THAT I WILL KNOW
WHEN TO NOT TRUST – I TRUST MY-
SELF THAT MUCH.

#48

I NEVER GOT
IN THERAPY THAT...

I CONSTANTLY CREATE
THE REALITY I LIVE IN.
IF I CAN CREATE THIS
SO EFFECTIVELY,
WITHOUT BEING AWARE THAT
I'VE CREATED THIS,
THINK OF WHAT I COULD CREATE
IF I REALLY PUT MY MIND TO IT!

#49

I NEVER GOT
IN THERAPY THAT...

SUBSTANCE ABUSE, AS WELL
AS OTHER ADDICTIVE PATTERNS
OF THOUGHT & BEHAVIOR
ARE JUST WAYS TO COPE WITH THE
INSANITY OF CONSENSUS REALITY.
IT MAKES SENSE TO ESCAPE THE
CRAZINESS, WHEN NO OTHER
SANE PATH APPEARS AVAILABLE.
MAKING SENSE OF THE CRAZINESS
IS THE FIRST STEP TO RECLAIM-
ING & EMPOWERING MYSELF INTO
GREATER DEGREES OF SANITY.

#50

I NEVER GOT
IN THERAPY THAT...

BLAMING MYSELF FOR MY
INADEQUATE STATE OF BEING
HINGES ON A REALITY THAT
FORGOT THAT I AM HUMAN.
MY EXISTENCE AS A HUMAN BEING
REQUIRES THAT I ALLOW &
ACCEPT MY INADEQUACIES,
BECAUSE I'VE CHOSEN
TO TAKE THIS FORM.
I SURRENDER MY BELIEF THAT
I'M SUPER HUMAN &
WITHOUT FALLIBILITY.

#51

I NEVER GOT
IN THERAPY THAT...

THE PROMISE I MADE TO MYSELF
TO REMAIN INVULNERABLE
IS A PROMISE I CANNOT KEEP.
IF I CONTINUE TO HOLD
MYSELF TO THIS PROMISE,
I WILL, IN ALL LIKELIHOOD,
BETRAY MYSELF AGAIN
& AGAIN & AGAIN.

#52

I NEVER GOT
IN THERAPY THAT...

VULNERABILITY IS
AN ASPECT OF THE HUMAN
EXPERIENCE THAT I HAVE
COME TO KNOW INTIMATELY.
I CAN TRUST,
THAT NO MATTER WHAT, I AM SAFE.

#53

I NEVER GOT
IN THERAPY THAT...

TO TOTALLY & COMPLETELY
LOVE & ACCEPT MYSELF
NO MATTER WHAT,
IS FOUNDATIONAL TO CREATING
A LIFE WORTH LIVING.
THIS LOVE & ACCEPTANCE OCCURS
WHEN I AM WILLING TO SEE THE
ROOT SOURCE OF MY MISTAKES
AS OCCURRING WAY BEFORE
I HAD THE WISDOM
TO KNOW THE DIFFERENCE.

#54

I NEVER GOT
IN THERAPY THAT...

MY PRACTICE
IS TO PURGE MYSELF
OF WHATEVER DOESN'T
ALLOW ME TO RECEIVE LOVE
IN ALL OF ITS ABUNDANCE.

#55

I NEVER GOT
IN THERAPY THAT...

WE ARE ALL ADDICTED,
IF NOT TO A SUBSTANCE,
THEN TO THE CHEMICALS
PRODUCED THROUGH
HABITUAL PATTERNS
OF THINKING & FEELING.
TRULY, WE ARE ALL RECOVERING
FROM THE HABIT OF SELF-HATING.

#56

I NEVER GOT
IN THERAPY THAT...

SPEAKING MY TRUTH
REQUIRES THAT I BE OPEN
TO HEARING WHAT I MAY NOT
WANT TO KNOW ABOUT ME.

#57

I NEVER GOT
IN THERAPY THAT...

ALL ADDICTIONS
ARE IN SERVICE TO
AVOIDING THE TRUTH.

#58

I NEVER GOT
IN THERAPY THAT...

THERE ARE MANY PATHS
& MANY TEACHERS,
& ONLY ONE TRUTH.
I AM THE ONLY ONE
WHO CAN DEFINE
THAT TRUTH FOR MYSELF.

#59

I NEVER GOT
IN THERAPY THAT...

MY HEALING & SENSE
OF WHOLENESS
ARISE FROM MY DEDICATION
TO BECOMING MY OWN GURU.

#60

I NEVER GOT
IN THERAPY THAT...

THERE IS NO SUCH THING
AS A SHADOW-SELF.
THERE IS ONLY ME –
THE ME I WISH TO BE,
& THE ME I'M SCARED TO BE.

#61

I NEVER GOT
IN THERAPY THAT...

BEING BOXED INTO A DIAGNOSIS
TELLS YOU WHAT YOU'VE BECOME,
PERHAPS.
IT DOESN'T CELEBRATE THE
BRILLIANCE THAT IT TOOK
TO CHOOSE TO CHOOSE ALL OF
WHAT IT TOOK TO BECOME THAT.

#62

I NEVER GOT
IN THERAPY THAT...

IF I'M SMART ENOUGH
TO BECOME THIS,
THEN I'M SMART ENOUGH
TO BE SOMETHING ELSE.

#63

I NEVER GOT
IN THERAPY THAT...

I AM NEVER NOT
A SPIRITUAL BEING.
I AM NEVER NOT BEING HUMAN.
CONVERSELY, I AM NEVER
MY CIRCUMSTANCES, OR EVEN MY
RESPONSES TO CIRCUMSTANCES.

#64

I NEVER GOT

IN THERAPY THAT...

WHEN I'M IN A DREAM,

I DON'T KNOW I'M DREAMING.

WHEN I AWAKEN,

I KNOW IT ALL TO BE AN ILLUSION.

THAT'S THE WAY LIFE IS.

#65

I NEVER GOT
IN THERAPY THAT...

WE ARE INCAPABLE
OF REALIZING TRUTH
BEYOND OUR OWN
LEVEL OF CONSCIOUSNESS.
IT SOMETIMES TAKES A DISASTER
OF SOME SORT, OR A TWO-BY-FOUR,
TO TAKE US TO THE NEXT LEVEL.
WHA-HOOO!

#66

I NEVER GOT
IN THERAPY THAT...

LIFE IS LEARNED
IN INCREMENTS –
ONE STEP AT A TIME.

#67

I NEVER GOT
IN THERAPY THAT...

THERE IS NO HURRY
BECAUSE THERE IS NOWHERE
FOR ME TO GO.
I'M ALREADY WHERE
I ALWAYS WANT TO BE.

#68

I NEVER GOT
IN THERAPY THAT...

TO SAY TO SOMEONE:
"TELL ME MORE,"
IS TO ENJOY THE RAPTURE
OF AN EXPERIENCE
YOU WILL NEVER EVER KNOW
EXCEPT THROUGH LISTENING.

#69

I NEVER GOT
IN THERAPY THAT...

WE ARE BORN
TO EXPERIENCE THE CAPACITIES
THAT WE THOUGHT WERE
SAVED FOR HOLY PEOPLE.
WE ARE ALL HOLY PEOPLE.
WE CAN ALL TALK WITH GOD
DIRECTLY, & WE CAN ALL HEAR
THE RESPONSE IN A HEARTBEAT
OF A HUMMINGBIRD.
IT ALL DEPENDS ON WHAT YOU
BELIEVE YOU ARE CAPABLE OF.

#70

I NEVER GOT
IN THERAPY THAT...

LOGIC & RATIONALIZATION
HAVE MANY LEVELS.
SPIRITUAL LOGIC MAY SEEM
TO CONFLICT WITH
MENTALIZATIONS.
THIS IS WHERE THE TRUE WORK
OF DISCERNMENT BEGINS.

#71

I NEVER GOT

IN THERAPY THAT...

I CANNOT CONTROL MY DESTINY

IF I'M UNWILLING

TO CONTROL MY THOUGHTS

& MY EMOTIONS.

#72

I NEVER GOT

IN THERAPY THAT...

MEDITATION IS A

TERRIFIC TOOL

TO TRAIN MY MIND

TO LET GO OF

WHAT ISN'T OF VALUE TO ME.

#73

I NEVER GOT

IN THERAPY THAT...

TRAINING MY MIND

TO STOP WHEN I SAY STOP

IS LIKE TRAINING A PUPPY.

FIRST I HAVE TO DECIDE

WHO IS IN CHARGE.

#74

I NEVER GOT
IN THERAPY THAT...

A GOOD THOUGHT PARTNER
EMPOWERS ME TO DISCOVER
& TO ACT ACCORDING TO
MY OWN TRUTH –
NOT TO MORPH INTO
THEIR PARTICULAR TRUTHS OR
THE TRUTH OF THE MASSES.

#75

I NEVER GOT
IN THERAPY THAT...

I CAN CHOOSE
TO DIRECT MY LIFE
BASED ON THE FEAR-MONGERINGS
OF MASS MEDIA,
OR I CAN CLEANSE MYSELF
OF FEAR-RELATED IMAGININGS
& CHOOSE FOR MYSELF
HOW TO DIRECT MY LIFE.

#76

I NEVER GOT
IN THERAPY THAT...

I CAN IMAGINE
WHATEVER I WANT –
& WHAT I WANT
IS
TO EXPERIENCE
PEACE, LOVE & SERENITY.

#77

I NEVER GOT
IN THERAPY THAT...

I'M THOROUGHLY INFLUENCED
BY THE COMPANY I KEEP.
THIS INCLUDES THE TV SHOWS
& MOVIES I WATCH,
& THE MUSIC & THE NEWS.
DO I FEEL GOOD
OR DO I FEEL BAD
THROUGH THE COMPANY I KEEP?

#78

I NEVER GOT
IN THERAPY THAT...

I HAVE TO BE IN
RIGHT-RELATIONSHIP
WITH MYSELF, FIRST,
BEFORE I CAN BE IN
RIGHT-RELATIONSHIP
WITH EVERYONE & EVERYTHING.

#79

I NEVER GOT
IN THERAPY THAT...

MY DESIRE FOR ROMANCE
WITH THAT SPECIAL SOMEONE
HAS TO BE WEIGHED AGAINST
OTHER DESIRES THAT
I ALSO HOLD DEAR:
FREEDOM, FLEXIBILITY, SOLITUDE,
UNCOMPROMISING PEACE.

#80

I NEVER GOT

IN THERAPY THAT...

LEARNING TO

WEIGH VALUES & PRIORITIES

SO THAT I CAN TRULY SERVE

MY HIGHEST TRUTH,

MY HIGHEST KNOWING

& MY HIGHEST GOOD,

TAKES TIME & COMMITMENT

AS WELL AS FIERCE DEVOTION

TO MY ESSENTIAL SELF.

#81

I NEVER GOT
IN THERAPY THAT...

IT'S NEVER ABOUT MONEY.
I FORGET THAT THE SOURCE
OF ALL CURRENCY IS ETERNAL.
I FORGET THAT
MY WEALTH HAS NO END.
I FORGET THAT I AM THE SOURCE.
I FORGET A LOT OF THINGS!

#82

I NEVER GOT
IN THERAPY THAT...

A MID-LIFE CRISIS
IS MOST LIKELY
AN EMERGENCE OF SPIRIT
TELLING ME TO
"GET ON WITH IT!
STOP FOOLING AROUND,
& LIVE LIFE FULLY!

#83

I NEVER GOT
IN THERAPY THAT...

MY WILL BE DONE!
ONLY THROUGH
DISCIPLINED DISCERNMENT
& DEEP INVESTIGATION
WILL I DISCOVER THE BELIEFS
& PERCEPTIONS FROM WHICH
MY LIFE, AS IT IS, HAS ARISEN.

#84

I NEVER GOT
IN THERAPY THAT...

MY LIFE AS IT IS,
IN THIS MOMENT,
IS THE COMPLETION
OF THE WORK TAKEN ON
BY MY WILL.
SO...

#85

I NEVER GOT
IN THERAPY THAT...

IF MY WILL BE DONE,
WHAT DO I
FERVENTLY WILL TO BE,
& BE DONE?

#86

I NEVER GOT
IN THERAPY THAT...

MEDITATION IS
A TOOL TO DEVELOP THE MUSCLES
OF REGULATING THOUGHT.
ONCE I GET THE HANG OF IT...
OH, THE PLACES I'LL GO!

#87

I NEVER GOT
IN THERAPY THAT...

THERE IS SO MUCH WONDER
OUTSIDE THE COGNITIVE WORLD
WE THINK IS REAL.

#88

I NEVER GOT
IN THERAPY THAT...

I AM MASTERFUL IN MY ABILITY
TO DECEIVE MYSELF & OTHERS.
I HAVE THE CAPACITY
TO MASTERFULLY
UNCONCEAL WHAT UNDERLIES
MY NEED TO DECEIVE.
DIG IN!

#89

I NEVER GOT

IN THERAPY THAT...

WHY DECEIVE?

TO PROTECT THE TRUE ME

AS LOVE & INNOCENCE.

I HAVE YET TO TRUST

THAT THIS IS MY SAVING GRACE.

NO DECEPTION REQUIRED.

#90

I NEVER GOT
IN THERAPY THAT...

MY FEAR OF EXPERIENCING THE
EMOTIONAL CHARGE OF BETRAYAL
INFLUENCES MY CHOICES
& MY CAPACITY TO BE IN PEACE
WITH ANY INDIVIDUAL
ON THE PLANET.

#91

I NEVER GOT
IN THERAPY THAT...

IN MY HOLINESS (WHOLENESS)
I AM SAFE.
IT IS ONLY MY RELENTLESS
GRASPING FOR INTERPRETATIONS
THAT HAS IT BE OTHERWISE.

#92

I NEVER GOT
IN THERAPY THAT...

MY DESIRE TO HELP,
SUPPORT & EMPOWER,
MORE OFTEN THAN NOT,
IS MY EGO'S ATTACHMENT
TO POWERFULLY CONTROLLING
THE OUTCOME
OF OTHER PEOPLE'S LIVES.

#93

I NEVER GOT
IN THERAPY THAT...

MY EGO IS RUTHLESS
IN ITS ATTEMPT TO
PROVE GOD WRONG.

#94

I NEVER GOT

IN THERAPY THAT...

ATTEMPTING TO RESOLVE
PROBLEMS ANYWHERE
BUT AT THEIR SOURCE
IS LIKE PUTTING A BAND-AID
ON A MALIGNANT TUMOR.
BUT WHERE IS THE SOURCE,
& HOW DO I DIVINE IT?

#95

I NEVER GOT
IN THERAPY THAT...

RELATIONSHIPS ARE ONLY
VEHICLES FOR LEARNING
RIGHT-RELATIONSHIP
WITH MYSELF.
I WILL NEVER STOP WANTING
TO LEARN, SO I'LL NEVER STOP
BEING IN RELATIONSHIPS.

#96

I NEVER GOT
IN THERAPY THAT...

I HAVE ALWAYS HAD,
& NOW HAVE,
THE CAPACITY TO EXCHANGE
ONE FORM OF IMAGINATION
FOR ANOTHER.
I MAKE BELIEVE
WHAT I CHOOSE
TO MAKE BELIEVE.

#97

I NEVER GOT
IN THERAPY THAT...

ONLY WHEN I'M READY
TO KNOW
WILL I BE READY TO GO.

#98

I NEVER GOT
IN THERAPY THAT...

THE WORLD
I THOUGHT WAS REAL
IS JUST A TINY SPECK
OF AN ENORMOUS REALITY,
WHICH CARRIES ME ALONG
ON THE RIDE OF EXPANSION
& WAKING UP.
NO ONE GETS LEFT BEHIND.

#99

I NEVER GOT
IN THERAPY THAT...

I AM ALWAYS
PROVIDED WITH
TWO CHOICES:
WILL I CHOOSE
BASED ON FEAR,
OR WILL I CHOOSE
BASED ON DARING TRUTH?

#100

I NEVER GOT
IN THERAPY THAT...

MY LIFE IS AN
EXTRAORDINARY ADVENTURE;
THE SOLE PURPOSE
BEING TO EXPERIENCE
THE EFFORTLESS EXPRESSION
OF DIVINE GRACE AS
ME,
MIRACULOUS EXISTENCE.

#101

ABOUT THE AUTHOR

Dr. Rosie Kuhn is an international life and business coach, trainer and speaker. She resides on Orcas Island in the San Juans with her sweet dog, Gracie. Contact Rosie via her website for coaching, training and/or speaking engagements.

www.theparadigmshifts.com

Are you interested in more products connected to this book and it's contents? Please go to:

www.inevergotfromtherapythat.com

MORE BOOKS BY DR. ROSIE KUHN

IF ONLY MY MOTHER HAD TOLD ME...
(OR MAYBE I JUST WASN'T LISTENING.)

YOU KNOW YOU ARE
TRANSFORMING WHEN...

DILEMMAS OF BEING IN BUSINESS

THE ABCS OF SPIRITUALITY IN BUSINESS

SELF EMPOWERMENT 101

THE UNHOLY PATH OF A
RELUCTANT ADVENTURER

Please visit **www.theparadigmshifts.com**
for more information and to purchase books.

CPSIA information can be obtained
at www.ICGtesting.com
Printed in the USA
FSOW01n0726301214
4231FS